D0426249

THE
HOLLYWOOD
DICTIONARY

TEXT BY TIMOTHY M. GRAY
ILLUSTRATIONS BY J C. SUARÈS

welcome
BOOKS

new york • san francisco

A *Variety*® Book
5700 Wilshire Blvd., Los Angeles, CA 90036
(323) 857-6600
www.variety.com

Published by Welcome Books®
An imprint of Welcome Enterprises, Inc.
6 West 18th Street, New York, NY 10011
www.welcomebooks.com

Publisher: Lena Tabori
Project Director: Katrina Fried

Designed by Bruce Brosnan

Copyright © 2005 Variety, Inc.
Variety is a registered trademark of Reed Elsevier
Properties Inc., and used under license. This book
and its contents are based upon *Variety* ® Slanguage.

All rights reserved. No part of this book may be reproduced or
utilized in any form or by any means, electronic or mechanical,
including photocopying, recording, or by any information storage or
retrieval system, without permission in writing from Variety, Inc.

Library of Congress Cataloguing-in-Publication Data on file
ISBN-10: 1-932183-78-7 / ISBN-13: 978-1-932183-78-8

Printed in Hong Kong
1 3 5 7 9 10 8 6 4 2

Scribe

INTRODUCTION

WHEN CRIMINALS PLOT a big job, they need to make sure that outsiders can't understand the conversation. So over the years they have come up with terms like "ice" for jewels and "pigeon" for victim, so that eavesdroppers can have no idea what they are talking about.

Thus slang is sometimes born out of necessity.

Moving from the criminal underworld to showbiz—which is more of a little hop than a jump—we find that people in the entertainment business have their own specialized argot. In this case, the jargon's not used to exclude people from important conversations, but as a shorthand for conveying ideas.

So a play has "legs." That one word quickly conveys the notion that the play has the potential for a long run and, by implication, can earn a lot of money.

Of course other groups use slang. The vocabulary of rappers and teenagers is constantly changing. (Interesting that over the years a word like "bad" can switch between meaning bad and good, while "cool" has sustained its definition for decades.)

The fact is that most professions and social constellations possess their own language. Square dancers know how to do-si-do, but most city slickers wouldn't be able to do one if their life depended on it.

People in the financial world toss around phrases like "discretionary funds," "forecast one," and "media-neutral market-sector organizations." They (and only they) understand immediately what's being talked about.

(Were Martians faced with the task of deciphering our language, they'd be hard put.)

Some newspapers look down on slang and refuse to sully their pages with such vulgarities, but they're missing the point. Slang is the language of the people.

Since its founding in 1905, *Variety* has proudly used showbiz slang, or *slanguage*.

There are a lot of reasons for this. First off, it saves time. Equally important is the exuberant way it expresses everyday realities in the frantic world of showbiz.

It also saves space in a newspaper to say a film is "boffo" rather than to say "it's doing extremely well at the box office."

There are countless reasons to use slang, but the bottom line is simple: Slanguage is fun. Once upon a time in the 1930s, *Variety* ran the headline "Sticks Nix Hick Pix," which meant that folks in the farmland rejected films about the farmland. You have to pity the serious newspaper that abstains from such inspired lunacy.

Is it pretentious for a group to have its own language? Not really. To be pretentious, you have to take yourself seriously, and it's clear that showbiz slanguage doesn't lay claim to any such significance.

You rarely hear anyone at a Hollywood party use terms like "veep" or "prexy" in conversation. But when they read the word, they know immediately what it means.

And while showbiz slanguage was not invented to exclude outsiders, most people scratch their heads when they hear terms like "upfronts," "cume," and "ankle."

This book is for all the head-scratchers out there.

Niche

THE
HOLLYWOOD
DICTIONARY

Academy

In most dictionaries, "academy" refers to an association of scholars, writers, and students. "The Academy" can also be the park near Athens where Plato founded his school of philosophy. In Hollywood, it's almost always the Academy of Motion Picture Arts & Sciences, home of Oscar. If you're in the TV biz, you may be referring to the Academy of Television Arts & Sciences, where Emmy resides. Either way, it's much more significant and prestigious than anything Plato ever came up with.

A.D.

Assistant director or, in theater, artistic director. Not Anno Domini.

A.D.D.

A chemical condition in which someone can't concentrate

A.D.

on a subject. The flourishing of this diagnosis may be directly linked to the flourishing of the remote-control device.

A.D.R.
A movie credit referring to Additional Dialogue Replacement, such as the background voices in a party scene. Not to be confused with A.D.D., which is—um, wait, what were we talking about?

Affil
An affiliate. A local station that has a deal with a network to air its programs. These are the stations that have no choice about airing stupid sitcoms or reality shows, but have autonomy when it comes to creating stupid news shows.

Alphabet web
ABC. Get it?

Ankle
Verb, meaning to exit. The term is neutral, meaning either the exec quit or was fired. The origin: The last thing you see as someone goes out the door is his ankle.

Anni
Anniversary. In Hollywood, it's an excuse to throw a party and take out ads congratulating yourself, or to reissue a film on DVD ("The 20th Anniversary of *Splash!*") In the context of eternity, such celebrations are minor blips. But in Hollywood, these things are . . . come to think of it, in Hollywood, they're minor blips as well.

Ankle

Arnie

A term of affection for the star, the governator, the phenomenon. It was coined by newspapers and tabloids because Cruise, Hanks, Crowe, and Gibson fit easily into headlines, but "Schwarzenegger" makes things a bit too cramped.

Arthouse

A movie theater that shows foreign or indie films that are deemed to be "art." (This is in stark contrast to plexes showing films that are popular and thus not art.)

Aud

Audience. Sometimes it seems like Hollywood is trying to beat the auds.

Aussie

A term of affection for anyone from Australia though Aussies don't always feel affection in said term.

Awards season

Roughly mid-November through late February. In the film biz, this is equivalent to Lent, Advent, the High Holidays, and Ramadan rolled into one: a period of agony and celebration. See also Kudos season.

Ax

Someone is axed, gets the ax, or awaits the ax. It's a noun or verb that conjures up vague images of Anne Boleyn and masked executioners, but is actually scarier: After all, you don't have to stand in the Hollywood unemployment line if your head's been lopped off.

Aud

Ayem

A slang version of the two little letters that signify morning. For some reason, no one writes out pee-em. Perhaps it looks a little too much like a body function.

Backend

Contrary to perception, image-conscious folk in Hollywood *love* big backends. That's because it refers to money. Big names often make deals with little money upfront but big backends that promise a big share of the revenue.

Bash

A party, fund-raiser, or event, which can be formal or informal. It's odd that the term suggests violence. After enough Hollywood parties, you'll understand why.

Best boy

This "boy" is a man or woman who assists the gaffer or key grip. He/she is responsible for the routing and coiling of power cables, a skill that is taught at too few film schools. Oddly, despite all the awards shows in Hollywood, there is little recognition for the best best boy.

Backend

BevHills

The 90210 city. The city of Rodeo Drive, Eddie Murphy's cop, the Hillbillies, *Down & Out*, *Slums*. BevHills was once considered a surefire box office attraction until *Troop Beverly Hills* and *Beverly Hills Ninja* put an end to that particular Hollywood fantasy.

Biopic

A biographical film. Not pronounced bi-OP-ic, but BI-o-pic. This film is occasionally scrupulously based on fact, but usually isn't. Or it can be "inspired" by someone's life, meaning their real life wasn't considered interesting enough without the addition of certain embellishments.

Biz

Conversational or *Variety* term for *the* business. *The* industry. "Are you in the biz?" means show business, not "Are you in the world of business?" The business section of most newspapers does *not* refer to show business.

Blighty

Britain. Showbizzers borrowed this term from World War I soldiers, who got it from the Hindu word *bilayati*, which means European. Basically, in Hollywood the term refers to the place where they make all those Merchant-Ivory pictures, though neither Merchant nor Ivory was born in Blighty. It's a wacky world, all right.

Biopic

Blockbuster

The term usually refers to the Holy Grail of film execs, a big-grossing picture. It can also refer to a picture with a big budget, irrespective of its B.O. Then of course there's the Blockbuster store, which rents pictures that were blockbusters. Originally a World War II bomb that could destroy a city street, this term now refers to something that destroys brain cells.

Blurb

An ad or a quote. The "Got milk?" blurbs are a big hit; alternatively, newspaper ads sometimes run blurbs from critics ("The laugh-out-loud comedy of the summer!"). Either way, these are things that bring joy to humdrum lives.

B.O.

Box office intake. When a headline says, "Summer B.O. at an All-Time High," it's not a reference to body odor.

Boffo

Variety term for terrific. No one knows how the term came into being, but it's fun to say.

Bomb

In the U.S., it means a fiasco. In the U.K., a big hit. In U.S. street slang, it's good if preceded by "da," as in "She's da bomb." Go figure.

Boom operator

The person who holds a microphone on a long stick over the actors' heads and (hopefully) out of camera

Blockbuster

range. It does not refer to the person responsible for blowing up the model of the White House in *Independence Day*. That would be the big-kaboom operator.

Bow

Launch, opening, debut, premiere. A film bows on two thousand screens. Since showbiz people usually take a bow when they're finished, this term makes no sense, but much about Hollywood makes no sense.

Buzz-to-dud

A sad trend that is pretty self-explanatory. Some productions start out with a lot of anticipation (due to either the people involved or the budget) and then fizzle. Producers and the media are alternatively scared and delighted by this. *Gigli* was hardly the biggest money-loser of all time, but the Ben-&-Jen media saturation gave a disproportionate amount of attention to this buzz-to-dud.

Certs

Certifications. A music industry term for optimism or for accomplishment, because a record is "certified" when it ships a half million copies. That's a lot. But that's not to

Buzz-to-dud

say it's *sold* a half million copies, just that the record company believes it will sell most of them. Ah, the dreams of showbiz.

Chopsocky
Variety coined this phrase in the 1970s about martial-arts movies. So *Crouching Tiger, Hidden Dragon* was a socko chopsocky.

Cleffer
A songwriter. Named for the clef note. Because "tuner" sounds like someone who's fixing your piano.

Coast
Los Angeles. People fly out to the Coast, and it's always the Pacific Coast, but never Oregon or even Northern California. There's only one small stretch of the Coast that really matters. (It's in the area of Malibu, home of mudslides, flooding and fires, and expensive stores—but at least it provides privacy.)

Coin
It's too vulgar to use the word "money," so people talk about the "coin" taken in.

Competish
Competition. Only used to describe other people, never oneself. An award nominee never admits he's in competish with other actors; he's honored to be in their company. An exec is never in competish with a colleague; they're happy to be working together.

Coin

Confab

A conference or gathering. Somehow, it makes the gathering sound more interesting.

Conglom

Conglomerate. There's no way to make this sound more interesting.

Corny

Variety helped popularize this word, which is a shorter version of "corn-fed." It originally referred to music that was country-style (i.e., unsophisticated). Pre–*O Brother, Where Art Thou?* this was considered a bad thing.

Credits

The list of contributors at the end of a show. The 1968 *2001: A Space Odyssey* concluded with a roster of 39 actors and 38 techies. The 1997 *Titanic* end credits list 93 actors, 67 companies, and 1,294 behind-the-scenes workers.

Crix

Critics. A profession in which people are paid good money to spout off their opinions about things (films, TV shows, music) on the supposition that they are somehow more qualified, more thoughtful, and more intelligent than the rest of us.

Cume

A film's cumulative take at the box office. The third *Lord of the Rings* had a worldwide cume of $1 billion. The term looks vaguely pornographic, but you get used to it.

Crix

D

Deejay or d.j.

Disc jockey. A term that encompasses those anonymous voices on the radio like the guy who is really energetic and wacky at 6 a.m. while his sidekick screams with laughter though all you want is some pleasant music to wake up to. It also encompasses those soft and friendly voices who announce the title and performer of every song except the one that you wanted to know about.

Demos

Demographics, not Democrats (i.e., the breakdown of a segment of the audience). E.g., some blurbs target the 18–54 demo. Studios like to target demos in the mistaken belief that they can justify a silly film or TV show because it was targeted to a key demo.

Diskery

Record company. This is slang, though with compact disks replacing vinyl, "diskery" seems a more precise term than "record company."

Distrib

Distributor. The company that releases the film. The company that has to put up with complaints from theater

Demos

owners, filmmakers, stockholders, and the public as it amasses its millions.

Docu

Documentary. Formerly a synonym for "sleep inducing." Now that documentaries are actually good, they are being touted as big-screen versions of reality television. This is progress.

Double pump

A network trick to lure viewers by showing a new series twice in one week, or once on the network and once on a cable affiliate. Actually, in the porno industry it may refer to something else, but we don't want to get into that right now.

D.P.

Director of photography or cinematographer. The man (or woman) responsible for making scenery look good and actors look even better.

Dupe

To duplicate a film (i.e., a print or DVD). Also, to deceive. In other words, a pirate might dupe people with dupes.

Dupe

Electile dysfunction

Variety coined the term to refer to the "hanging chads" fiasco in the 2000 Florida election. Now it refers to any election mishap. What did you think it meant?

Exec

Executive. A term of great importance or of no value, depending on who uses it. If it's used to describe someone else, it's positive. If someone describes himself as an exec or executive, you can be pretty sure he is a self-employed jerk with high aspirations.

Exhib

Exhibitor (i.e., theater owner). In theory, a man who is in the business of showing movies in state-of-the-art settings; in truth, it's a man who's in the business of selling popcorn and soda for as much money as he can get away with.

Eye web

CBS, because its logo is a big stylized eyeball. It used to be called the Tiffany network, but now that kinda denotes snobbery. Now, when it's good, it's the Aye-Aye! network. When it's bad, it's the Ay-ay-ay! Network.

Exhib

Feevee

A blanket term referring to pay-cable webs such as HBO and Showtime (i.e., fee TV). Conventional wisdom says these feevee services have better programs because they're not fettered by network censors or Madison Avenue concerns. This is one of those rare instances where conventional wisdom is correct.

Femme

A woman. In olden times (the 1930s and '40s), women were routinely described with such terms as chick, bimbo, babe, and femme. Now "femme" is generally considered to be the only non derogatory word of the bunch. Well, at least by most femmes.

First-dollar

The best sort of film deal, reserved for only primo actors, directors, or producers, who get a share of every cent that a film makes. In squishier contracts, the participant would only get money after the film "makes a profit," but creative accounting ensures that even a megablockbuster never makes a profit.

Feevee

First-look

A studio signs a deal to get the first opportunity to buy a project. If Hollywood is a theoretically grown-up version of childhood, this is the adult way of saying, "I've got dibs on Julia Roberts!"

Flack

A vaguely contemptuous term for publicists, who are always the object of vague contempt in H'wood.

Floppola

Worse than a flop. Comparable to a (U.S.) bomb.

Flyovers (or flyover states)

Anything between California and New York (i.e., a state you would fly over, but never visit—or at least you'd never admit you visited).

Foley artist

The people who do sounds of footsteps and other incidental noises. Named for Jack Foley, who worked in the early days of talkies.

Fotog

Photographer. There are pros on the set who snap "candid" moments, there are fotogs who airbrush stars to perfection, and then there are stars who want to feel artistic so they publish a book of their exquisite snapshots.

Frog

The WB netlet. Named for its mascot, Michigan J. Frog, a dancing amphibian. Draw your own conclusions about the aspirations of the netlet.

Floppola

F/X

Effects, or visual effects. In olden times (i.e., the 1990s), a film was described as an f/x film if it had a lot of visual effects. Now CGI has ensured that virtually every film is an f/x film.

G

Grand, or $1,000. "The pic's cume at one theater is 50G for two weeks." It was once thought of as a grand sum. Now it's petty cash.

Gaffer

An electrician responsible for lighting on a film or TV set. When the d.p. says, "Let there be light," everybody turns to the gaffer.

Gaul

France. The country of Cannes, Catherine Deneuve, Gaulois cigarettes, and the grand artistry of Renoir and Truffaut. It's also the country that embraces Woody Allen and Quentin Tarantino, so you gotta wonder what's in the wine those guys are drinking.

Gaul

Gong

In the U.S., you get a gong when the audience rejects you. In the U.K., you get a gong when you are given an award. See also Bomb to understand the heart-breaking non communication between America and Britain.

Gotham

An old-style term for New York City. It was used by U.S. newspapers even before Batman started prowling around Gotham City.

Greenlight

The firm go-ahead for a project. In car-obsessed Los Angeles, it's not surprising that "greenlight" has become a concept of ultimate affirmation.

Grip

A person who has varied duties on a set, such as setting up equipment or moving props. If someone in Hollywood says, "Get a grip," they're not telling you to calm down. Well, *maybe* they're not.

H

Hardtop

A fading term for an indoor theater, whether a single-

Gotham

screen or a plex, meant to distinguish it from a drive-in.

Helmer

Director. Because he's at the helm of the ship, so to speak.

Honcho

A big shot. From the Japanese word *hancho*, meaning group leader. Didn't know that, did you?

Hoofer

Dancer. Though a "hoofer" sounds like a clumsy oaf compared to a "terp," these folks are just as agile.

Horse opera

Western. At one time, there were so many Wild West films and TV shows being made, showbiz invented various terms to keep the word "Western" from getting stale. Despite the occasional Tom Selleck telefilm and HBO's "Deadwood," there is no such danger these days.

HQ

Headquarters. It was once slang, but James Bond movies helped make "HQ" acceptable. And, besides, "headquarters" can be a confusing term, as when the 99¢ Store bills itself as "your back-to-school headquarters!"

Huddle

A conference, or preliminary meeting. From the football term, though showbiz huddles involve a type of violence that's more psychological than physical.

Hoofers

HUT

Homes Using Television. When network execs realized that their viewers at any given hour represented only a small portion of the number of people living in the U.S., they got depressed. So they decided to measure viewers by the number of HUTs, which was kinda comforting.

Hype

To exaggerate the worth of something you're trying to sell. It's a noun or verb, and a useful term in showbiz.

Hyphenate

Someone who is so great, he cannot confine his talent to one area, so becomes a hyphenated talent: e.g., writer-director, actor-poet. Alternatively, someone who is moderately talented in one area, but parlays that into a career as professional dabbler in other areas.

I

IA

Short for the International Alliance of Theatrical Stage Employees. "Stage" in the sense of "soundstage." No jokes here. Nobody makes jokes about unions in Hollywood.

HUT

Indie

An independent, whether it's a film, production company, whatever. The term either connotes admiration ("That Steven Soderbergh has the indie spirit!") or condescension ("*My Big Fat Greek Wedding* did very well for an indie").

Ixnay evernay

Emphatic, pig-Latin version of "Nix! Never!" Not frequently used, but a real attention-grabber when it's shouted out in the middle of a meeting.

Journo

Journalist. The most sublime occupation imaginable. The glamour, the respect! Journalists are members of the fourth estate, and are always trying to figure out who's living in those other three estates.

Journos

K

Kidvid
TV show aimed at children, meaning a TV show that's unwatchable for anyone with an IQ over seventy.

Kiwi
Anyone from New Zealand. From the kiwi bird, which lives in that region. It's a term that became immediately fashionable after Peter Jackson's success.

Kudo
An award. Oscar is the king kudo. From the Greek *kudos*, for glory or renown. Yes, it's actually only used in plural form, but if "sitcom" and "veep" can become words, so can "kudo."

Kudocast
A televised awards show. The Golden Globes are a kudocast; the DGA Awards are not.

Kidvid

L

Legit
Live theater. It's often called "legitimate theater," a holdover from the days when it needed to be distinguished from vaudeville.

Legs
A movie or play that is long running. *Cats* had great legs, because it ran for eighteen years. It was a little sacrilegious, but true nonetheless, when *Variety* said that *The Passion of the Christ* had great legs.

Lense
Verb meaning to film. "'The Sopranos' lenses in New Jersey." It only refers to film, not to videotape, though still fotogs (i.e., photographers) are sometimes called lensmen.

Longform (archaic)
A telepic or miniseries. The term is still used, but not often, mostly because networks are not as enamored of TV movies as they once were, and the era of sixteen-hour miniseries is a thing of ancient history.

Legit

M

Made-for
A telefilm. It's a short version of "made-for-television," but it doesn't refer to a series.

Mag hag
Anyone who's into magazines or the magazine business. This term applies to men and women equally and thus is not a sexist term for Tina Brown or Bonnie Fuller.

Majors
A loosely used term to describe the Hollywood studios. "Studio" usually means a place with a backlot and soundstages, but then United Artists became a big "studio" without any backlot, so people started using "the majors." Now people with megabucks announce a film slate and claim to be "an instant major." They rarely are.

Megabuck
Adjective to describe any project that costs a lot of money. In Hollywood, this can refer to anything from an epic film to a pricey lunch.

Major

Megaplex

A multiplex with more than sixteen screens, which means a place where you can pay admission for one film and sneak into several others, or a place where a kid can buy a ticket to a PG toon and then go into the gorefest at the theater across the hall. It's a land of filmgoing opportunity.

Meller

Old Yeller was a meller, which is an archaic noun for "melodrama," itself a vague term to describe everything from *Uncle Tom's Cabin* to a Douglas Sirk flick to "The O.C."

Mini-major

DreamWorks, Focus Features, and New Line are considered mini-majors because they don't have studio backlots and are not MPAA members, but their output is often bigger than "the majors." So why are they considered "mini"? It's one of the infinite mysteries of the universe.

Mitting

Applause. Because audience members clap their mitts together.

Modesty

No known definition; word unknown in Hollywood.

Mogul

A honcho or mega-exec or richly influential person. From the Mogul Empire, a Mongolian Muslim dynasty in India. People think Hollywood types are crass and

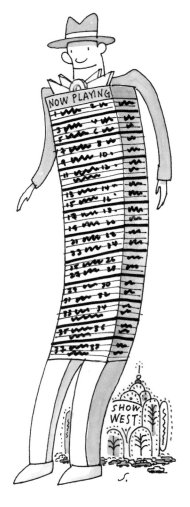

Megaplex

unsophisticated, but they describe themselves in terms pinched from Muslim dynasties and Japanese warrior culture. Gotta love that.

Moppet
A child actor, one of the most endearing and adorable life-forms on the planet. At least from a distance.

MOS
A scene is shot MOS when it's lensed without synchronized sound. Legend has it that the term was coined by a German cinematographer working in Hollywood in the late 1920s who declared the scene would be shot "mit-out sound."

Mouse House
Disney, the house that Mickey built, the land of Snow White, Hayley Mills, *Pirates of the Caribbean*, and, once upon a time, Michael Eisner. This is the company that gave rise to Mouseketeers Britney Spears, Christina Aguilera, and Justin Timberlake. In other words, it has a rich cultural heritage.

MPAA
Motion Picture Association of America, a coalition of the major studios that pay dues, get together to deal with common concerns, and hire a spokesman-advocate, which for thirty years was Jack Valenti. This group is the Hollywood equivalent of Mount Olympus.

Mouse House

Multiplex

A movie theater with seven to fifteen screens. Any fewer would qualify as a miniplex. Obviously, having "only" six screens is considered small potatoes. For something even more impressive, see Megaplex.

Narrowcast

A TV show or cable channel aimed at specific audiences. In other words, they don't have hopes of reaching many viewers. It's always good to know your limits.

Netlet

Usually a reference to UPN or the WB. Networks that don't air the same fare seven days a week or are in a limited number of markets. However, netlets generally hate being called "netlets," but it's not the worst thing those guys have been called.

Net TV

Network. Some East Coast snobs may say there's nothing good on TV, but look at "Masterpiece Theater," "The Honeymooners," "The Avengers," "Hill Street Blues," "Nightline," "The Simpsons," "The Sopranos," and "Andy Richter Controls the Universe."

Narrowcast

Niche

A genre that targets a narrow aud. See also Demos and Narrowcast. Come to think of it, Hollywood has an awful lot of terms for the concept of "low ambitions."

Nitery

Nightclub. A word that conjures up glamorous 1940s orchestras and ballroom dancing and gangsters, but that currently is used to describe hip-hop and rave gatherings. Don't romanticize the past. Even in those 1940s niteries, people were passing out and barfing and getting into fistfights.

Nix

Reject. *Variety*'s headline "Sticks Nix Hick Pix" meant audiences in rural America were rejecting the films about people in rural America. An example of a headline outliving the phenomenon it was reporting.

Nom

Nomination for an award. Meryl Streep, for example, has a slew of Oscar noms; she somehow gloms onto noms.

Non-pro

Anyone who's not in showbiz. This refers to everyone from sanitation workers to nurses to dogcatchers to Nobel Prize poets. Even though they're professionals in their own field, to showbiz they're non-pros.

Niche

n.s.g.

Not so good. Archaic. *Variety* used the term until compassionate editors got tired of answering phone calls from eager actors saying, "I'm so excited to be mentioned in *Variety*! The reviewer said, 'I'm n.s.g.' What does that mean?"

Nut

Not what you'd think. It's the operating expense of a theater.

O&O

Owned & operated. National networks can own and operate a limited number of local stations. These are the network's O&Os. Sometimes they're boffo. Sometimes the O&O is n.s.g.

Oater

A Western. Because horses eat oats, and "hayer" was too difficult to say.

n.s.g.

Off-net

A show in syndication. Example: "After its network run, 'Friends' had big off-net success."

Org

Organization. Anything from the Academy to the Flat Earth Society. No judgments.

OTT

Over the top. Can refer to anything from a Prince performance to a John Waters film to Courtney Love's private life.

Oz

Australia. If you slur your pronunciation of the continent, you'll see how the term was coined. Directors Peter Weir (*Gallipoli*, *Witness*, *Master & Commander*) and Baz Luhrmann (*Strictly Ballroom*, *Moulin Rouge*) are genuine wizards of Oz.

Ozoner

A drive-in theater, i.e., a place where you can see a movie and remnants of the ozone layer at the same time.

OTT

P

P&A

Print and advertising. A budget to purchase hype when a film is released. Not to be confused with P.A., which refers to personal appearance, personal assistant, public address. An all-purpose abbreviation in showbiz.

Pact

A contract, usually written—though oral pacts are exceedingly (and inexplicably) popular in Hollywood. To quote Samuel Goldwyn, an oral contract is as good as the paper it's written on.

Passion Pit

(aka ozoner) Drive-in theater. Hey, the Laplanders have dozens of words for snow. Why shouldn't we have several terms for something that no one talks about?

Payola

Bribery, usually used to describe payment to deejays to get increased record play. A term that was shocking in the 1950s and 1960s. But in the age of Enron, this notion is about as startling as a rumble seat.

Pact

Peacock

NBC, named for the network's logo-mascot. It's a beautiful bird. Which is great if you want to have a bird as a mascot, as opposed to a frog or an eyeball.

Pen

Verb, meaning to write (e.g., "He's going to pen the next Harry Potter.") Hollywood writers will tell you that it has no relation to the noun "pen," as in "he's in the pen," as in prison, a place where you are cooped up and going stir crazy. They are all liars.

Pic

Motion picture. (Plural: pics or pix.) No one wanted to call it a "mo" or a "mo-pic."

Pour

Noun, meaning a cocktail party. A term used before health-conscious Hollywood stopped drinking alcohol, except maybe one glass of red wine a day because doctors say it's good for you. "Pour" can, however, refer to the pouring of mineral water, a much more acceptable pastime at a pour.

Powwow

Same as a huddle, but it's one more way in which Hollywood *honors* Native Americans.

Peacock

PPV

Pay per view. A system by which couch potatoes pay $39.95 to watch a longer "grudge" version of wrestling matches that they normally watch for free.

PR

See Praisery.

Praisery

See PR.

Preem

Premiere. Either a verb or noun. A word that connotes excitement to anyone outside of Hollywood and shrugs of "Eh, it's work" to anyone in showbiz.

Prexy or prez

President. It's a great job, because you get credit for the smart moves of your underlings and predecessors, while you can blame any mistake on the marketing department.

PPV

Product

Rather callous term used frequently to describe the output of a studio or network: "They have great product this year." This is why studio moguls don't consider their films as fodder for "arthouses."

Promo

Promotion. A notion that is part of the DNA of showbiz.

Props

An object to be handled by actors, such as a newspaper or teacup. Alternatively an abbreviated word for "proper respect," as in "You have to give her props for being a hard worker." It's yet another slang word co-opted by Caucasians in their rather feeble attempt to be hip-hop hip.

Pubcaster

Public broadcaster (i.e., a network that receives funds from the government and from generous donations by people like you). It's a network that shows "Sesame Street" and "Antiques Roadshow" and doo-wop group reunions but that conservatives try to remove funding from, because once a year they'll air a documentary on a gay couple or something.

Product

Q Scores

A company that measures the audiences recognition of, and affection for, various celebs. A high Q Score is a good thing. No relation to IQ scores.

Quadrant

The movie biz has identified four quandrants of filmgoers. *Mona Lisa Smile* is made for women under 25. *Something's Gotta Give* is for women over 25. *Dawn of the Dead* is aimed at men under 25. *The Alamo* is targeted at men 25-and-older. The ideal is a movie that everyone will love: A four-quadrant movie (*Titanic, The Lord of the Rings, Finding Nemo*). We're not making this stuff up, you know; people in Hollywood really do think like this.

R&B

Rhythm and blues. It's a concept that musicians (often white) invoke when they claim to be channeling the spirit of classic forebearers (often dead).

R&B

Reality

A concept that is hard to comprehend in Hollywood. Instead, it's used to describe television shows.

Rentals

The portion of a film's box office that is returned to the studio. Also used to describe summer homes in Malibu.

Rep

Representative, or agent, or manager. In Hollywood, you can't live without them, but you also can't live without complaining about them.

Retro

A style from the past. In Europe, this can refer to a former century or even millennium; in Hollywood, it refers to anything more than four years ago.

Reup

To renew a contract. Logically, it should be reink or repact. Go figure.

Rep

SAG

Screen Actors Guild. A union of actors who are always in the midst of negotiations that are highly dramatic because, frankly, they're actors.

Scatter

TV network ad time left over after upfront sales are made. Alternatively, a jazz vocalist.

Scribe

Writer. Can be a scripter or a journo. On Broadway and in the TV world, the scribe is venerated. In the film biz, uh, well, a little less so.

Scripter

Screenwriter. Gets less respect but a lot more money than other types of scribes.

Seg

Segment. Usually refers to one episode of a TV series. Occasionally an actor will take out an ad referring to "a very special episode," which means the actor gets to cry and pray in the seg and is hoping for an Emmy.

Sell-through

A homevideo that's priced to be bought by consumers (i.e., $10–$30). When homevideos started, they were priced about

Sell-through

$80 each, so a store would buy each copy and make back its money by renting them out; few consumers bought them. Now the studios are into sell-through. This whole video world follows the American tradition of always experimenting with ways to give the customers the minimum bang for the maximum buck.

Sesh

Session. When reporting box office grosses, it usually refers to a week; in music, it refers to one long session.

Showbiz

What we live for. What makes the world go round. What lights up our life. What puts the wind beneath our wings. The business we call show. The show we call business. You get the picture.

Shutter

Verb, meaning to close. A show, such as a Broadway play, metaphorically closes its shutters. Which causes shudders.

Sitcom

Situation comedy. The term usually refers to an American show; a situation comedy from the U.K. is a Britcom. One that does well is a hitcom.

Sked

Schedule. It can refer to a studio's release sked (when it opens what film), a network's prime-time sked (when it schedules its dramas and sitcoms), or even the day's events on an exec's BlackBerry (pitch session, lunch at The Grill, Pilates, shrink, etc.).

Showbiz

Skein

A TV series. The word actually means a loose bundle of yarn or thread. And what is a TV series if not a loose bunch of yarns?

Soap opera (or soap; also, sudser)

Variety coined this term in the 1930s, since radio dramas were sponsored by soap companies. And they've been in a lather ever since.

Socko

Terrif. Maybe even better than boffo. But clearly not as good as whammo.

Solon

A lawmaker. *Variety* uses this term and it's considered slang, but Solon was actually an Athenian statesman around 600 B.C. So clearly, slang is sometimes more hoity-toity and eggheady and precise than people think.

Spec

A TV special. Alternatively, a spec script. See below and weep.

Spec script

A spec script is written on speculation (i.e., the writer works without pay in the hope it will be sold). Hollywood is filled with such quaint, far-fetched notions.

Spec script

SRO

Standing room only. This comes from an old Broadway tradition: When all the seats were sold, they would say that there were tickets only in the standing room areas. It's hard to believe you needed such a complicated explanation.

Stuntman

When a lead character does a dangerous action, the stuntman performs the deed. However, some thesps have been known to boast that they do their own stunts. Aren't actors adorable sometimes?

Syndie

Noun referring to the syndication business or a show that's in syndication. This encompasses everything from Ellen DeGeneres's talkshow to "Jerry Springer" to "The Simpsons" reruns to "Xena: Warrior Princess." It even includes "Wheel of Fortune," but there will be no jokes here at the expense of that particular show. It's an easy target.

T

Tab mag

A tabloid magazine. Now it refers to benign shows like "Extra!" and "Access Hollywood," but the 1990s

Tab mag

marked the heyday of loud tab mags like "Current Affair" and "Inside Edition." Ah, those were the golden days of television.

Telefilm

Telepic. A movie made expressly for television—or one that was made for theatrical distribution, couldn't find a buyer, and was premiered on TV as if that was always the makers' intention.

Tenpercentery

Talent agency. Technically, they don't always take ten percent, but you're too far along in this book to be literal, aren't you?

Terp

(see also Hoofer) A dancer. From Terpsichore, Muse of lyric poetry and dance. Oddly, showbiz doesn't have a slang word for someone who practices lyric poetry.

Thesp

Actor. From the Greek Thespis, actor who stepped out of the chorus and went solo, paving the way for every actor since. Thank God for Thespis! Otherwise, what would "Entertainment Tonight" talk about?

Thrush

Female singer. From the bird. The term is not too popular these days, since it also refers to lesions of the mouth.

Tix

Tickets. A useful term for anyone writing headlines, since it rhymes with pix, hicks, nix, and kicks.

Thesp

Toon

Cartoon. Though "cartoon" can refer to a Leonardo drawing, a Batman comic, or a Popeye short, "toon" in showbiz is an animated thing that appears on TV or the big screen. None of that highfalutin Da Vinci stuff.

Topper

Honcho, big enchilada, mogul, maven, big cheese, numero uno, the person on top.

Tubthump

Promote. From the medieval practice of street performers banging on tubs to get attention. Some things never change.

Tuner

A musical. *Chicago* was a tuner. *Beauty and the Beast* was a toon tuner.

Turnaround

A project that is available after a studio has spent money on developing it—as long as the potential buyer reimburses the studio for its outlay.

Two-hander

A film or play for two actors. It has a completely different meaning in the porn world.

Tyro

A novice. From the Latin *tiro*, meaning recruit. Hey, don't take our word for it, look it up in a *real* dictionary.

Tuner

U

Upfront
Payment for the fall TV season made months in advance, when ad folk mistakenly believe that if a network scheduled the show, it must be good. An ironic term, considering that no one involved is upfront about the whole thing.

V

Veep
(veepee, VP, vice prez, or vice prexy) Vice president. Acquiring this title is a crucial step in any Hollywood career: Once you become veepee, you get your own parking space.

Vid
Noun, usually referring to homevideo (i.e., tapes or DVDs), but it can also refer to anything on tape (i.e., "Regis and Kelly," etc.)

Vid

Web

A network. Well, at least that's what it meant for decades. Now it means the Internet, as in World Wide Web and Webheads.

Weblet

Same as a netlet.

Whammo

Boffo, slammo, swell, terrif. But even better, if that's possible.

Wicket

Box office, or any place of admission. From a fairly obsolete English term for a small door or gate. So when Hugh Grant says something is a bit of a sticky wicket, you now know what he means.

Wiggle opera

Variety's 1920s term for a burlesque show, i.e., wiggling on a grand scale. In the sense that "Baywatch" is a jiggle opera, *Shrek* is a squiggle opera, and Chris Rock performing standup is a giggle opera. The opportunities are endless.

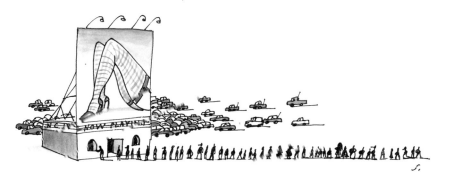

Whammo

Wrap

It's over. The end. Finito. You cry, then you move on to something else. Or else you go back to the beginning and start over again.

X-factor

An unpredictable ingredient that could ruin your plans or could make no impact at all. Since it applies to nearly every showbiz realm—prime-time TV schedules, B.O. weekends, Oscar races, etc.—Hollywood could be considered the X-factory. Not to be confused with "X-Files," "Fear Factor," or Max Factor.

Yakker

A primo example of showbiz onomatopoeia. This refers to shows in which people talk, such as "The Tonight Show," "The View," and "David Letterman." ("Yakker" can also refer to talkshows dealing with "real" people, such as "Oprah" and "Jerry Springer.")

Zitgeist

The youth culture. In youth obsessed Hollywood, the Holy Grail is an ability to tap into the zitgeist.

Zitgeist